CHAMPIO
HONOUR

John Ludden

The five games Real Madrid played to help out Manchester United after the Munich air disaster.
1959-1962

JOHN LUDDEN

ALL RIGHTS RESERVED

It was with a heavy heart that Real Madrid treasurer Don Raimondo Saporta broke the news of the Munich air crash to Alfredo Di Stefano. On hearing Saporta telephoned the player at his home. A call which the player would later recall as amongst the "Saddest moments of his life." As news reached Madrid of the horrific full extent of the disaster, a distressed President Don Santiago Bernabéu spoke solemnly of this great tragedy and of his prayers for the dead and the survivors. None more than so than his great friend Matt Busby, who by God's grace had survived the crash but now hung on for dear life in the Rechts Der Isar hospital in Munich. Twice to be given the last rites. Of the eleven Manchester United players who originally lined up against the Madrileños in the two-legged semi-final the previous season, five were killed instantly; Roger Byrne, David Pegg, Eddie Colman, Tommy Taylor and Liam Whelan, while Duncan Edwards fought on valiantly but lost his battle a few weeks later. Edwards' death touched Alfredo Di Stefano immensely and he told of the "Magnificent impression" Duncan Edwards had made on him during the second-leg in Manchester. "Such will to win and power in one so young. None deserved more the fullness of a great career than Duncan." What truly moved Di Stefano was being told how in his last ailing days, Edwards had called out for his gold watch presented to him in Madrid by Santiago Bernabéu following the semi-final in Madrid. It was a gift cherished by Edwards and after a swift investigation, a taxi was sent to the crash site, where astonishingly it still lay amongst the debris, and was returned to its rightful owner. Placed into his hand the watch for a short period appeared to have a revitalising effect on the player. Sadly, such was the extent of Edward's internal injuries that he passed away in the early hours of Friday 21st February 1958. His solid gold watch nearby calling time on a footballing colossus respected and feared by the Madrileños.

Now, six and eight in all of the players lay dead. Los chicos, the Busby Babes were gone.

In an act of wonderful generosity, the three times European champions offered to hand the grieving Mancunians the European cup for that season but whilst stricken in despair United politely refused, thanking in turn the Spaniards for their deep friendship. For this trophy had suddenly become so much more for all concerned with Manchester United and had to be one fought for and won. Too much blood had already been spilt, too many hearts had been broken to accept such an offer. There was also much talk of Bernabéu loaning United the services of Di Stefano for a season with the Madrid club paying half his exorbitant wages. Whilst it was claimed the player was willing, again the Old Trafford club baulked. Whether through pride or rumours that the petty pen pushers and insular attitudes of the Football League would refuse point blank the notion of a foreigner taking the place of a British player, it was hard to tell.

Football League chairman Alan Hardaker's words to Jimmy Murphy, 'Why go to Spain, why not boys from Manchester or the Black country where you found Edwards?'

Perhaps more disturbing was the League's shabby at best decision to ban United from competing in the 1958-59 European cup competition, after being invited by UEFA as a grateful thank you for their "Service to Football." Some statement that. United gratefully accepted and found themselves drawn against Swiss champions Young Boys of Berne, only then to be informed that their participation had been denied by the English hierarchy because they were not League champions. Again, another spiteful payback by Hardaker for Matt Busby going against his initial wishes to originally compete in the tournament. One he allegedly said was full of 'wogs and dago's.' Typically, Busby saw through such bile and United went ahead without his so-called blessing.

But despite such ill feelings directed towards them on home soil, there was one willing to help in any manner possible. In Madrid, Spanish hearts went out to the Mancunians in their darkest hour. In an act of extraordinary support, they came up with a special memorial pennant. It was conferred by Real Madrid to commemorate the destroyed English team and was entitled:

"Champions of Honour."

On it read the names of the dead players of which all considerable proceeds were sent to Old Trafford soon as collected. A further show of Real's nobility of spirit came that same summer when they contacted Manchester United offering free holidays in Spain to Munich survivors with all expenses paid. Madrid also provided for the injured players to use their sporting medical facilities. Some of the finest in the world. Again, all for no cost. Finally, and most importantly, a series of matches between the two clubs were swiftly arranged. Santiago Bernabéu not only agreeing to Matt Busby's plea for help but waived the normal £12,000 appearance fee charged by the Spaniards. A meeting took place in Madrid between Busby and Bernabéu where the United manager asked if they would consider accepting reduced fees, due to the cataclysmic effect the crash had placed upon his club. A generous Bernabéu insisted that the cash strapped United should, "Pay us what you can afford." With the Mancunians out of Europe and severely weakened, Busby realised how vital it was they retained the experience of playing against the world's best. Therefore, both men agreed to treat the games as serious affairs. A shake of hands and the deal was done. Five in all and each would prove to be laden rich with goals galore, memorable and truly fitting occasions for those no longer able to adorn the red shirt and partake.

UNITED. After a remarkable 1958-59 season during which Manchester United defied all odds to finish in runners-up position, many supporters were fooled into thinking business as usual and not the nightmare forecasted following Munich. Then, reality hit like a punch in the face. A new day truly dawned. The Mancunians had begun the 1959-60 campaign in more manic fashion, lying in sixth position at the time of Real Madrid's first visit. The previous Saturday they had been taken apart 4-0 at Preston North End whom, inspired by veteran, but still magical Tom Finney, were unlucky not to reach double figures. United were terrible as the wheels came off a half decent start to the campaign in gruesome style. Whilst dazzling going forward, defensively they were atrocious. Busby was desperate for reinforcements before a bad run morphed into a relegation battle. Fine defenders such as the late great Blackpool's Jimmy Armfield, and Rangers Eric Caldow were targeted without success. He also bid for Burnley's creative

Northern Irish midfielder Jimmy McIlroy, but a move was turned down by chairman Bob Lord with a warning to the Mancunians not to return. Lord had little sympathy for United after Munich and hardly appreciated them attempting to take his best player from Turf Moor. The previous season Jimmy Murphy's patched up team had gone down quite literally fighting in a 3-0 defeat at Burnley and Lord was quick after to condemn them. His description of them as 'Teddy boy's' did not sit well with Jimmy. But worse was his other comment. "There is too much sentiment about Manchester United. All the talk about Munich seems to have gone to the heads of the young players." It was the second time Busby had gone for McIlroy, the first time just before the crash. He would not go back again. After such words Lord turned United supporters' stomachs.

These were worrying times, at this stage of their recovery, a season where United veered from the sublime to the ridiculous on a weekly basis was driving supporters to despair. Following United had never been for the faint hearted, and that particular period they were capable of anything. Whether it be brilliant or absolutely shocking.

A thrilling goal-laden 6-3 win at Stamford Bridge over Chelsea watched by 66,000 evoked the best of memories pre-Munich. As did a 6-0 home crushing of Leeds. Then, the dark side, a new phenomenon;

a humiliating 5-1 drubbing at Old Trafford by Spurs and a feeble 3-0 surrender in the Manchester derby in which City outfought their neighbours was dreadfully hard to stomach. As the inconsistency stretched into October there were many worried brows on the Old Trafford terraces. A new dawn had arrived, this was the new United.

The grim expectation that the Munich survivors; Bobby Charlton, Harry Gregg, Bill Foulkes, Albert Scanlon and Dennis Viollet would carry the team were huge and unfair but all shown incredible bravery. Their every waking day must have still been filled with terrible images of friends lost and what they witnessed, and yet all carried on. Kept a red flag flying…Somehow. None more than Charlton, on whose slim young shoulders United fans placed most faith and the pressure was therefore the greatest. His best friends killed, Bobby found from somewhere the courage to not look back. He was regarded as one who spanned the pre-and post-Munich era. A living and breathing epitaph for the fallen who evoked the spirit of the Babes. With him around the future remained palatable. If their Bobby could go on then they also. In reality, Bobby Charlton's heart was broken and would never mend. Even today it remains obvious part of him is still on that infernal runway.

It was hoped that Real Madrid's imminent arrival

in Manchester would provide a welcoming change from the weekly pitfalls of First Division football. Pressure off, a friendly match with nothing at stake. Just take a deep breath, relax and enjoy the football of a Madrid team whom would simply go through the motions. Alas for the Mancunians it was not to be. President Bernabéu had instructed his players to do as what he and Busby agreed. Little did the Mancunians know what was set to hit them.

GAME ONE

Under orders from the boss to perform at full throttle and on £50 a man win bonus, Real Madrid came to Manchester and cut loose in terrifying manner. United received a dose of cruel reality as they were handed a footballing lesson, the 6-1 score-line saw them get off lightly and did little justice to the imperious Madrileños that night as Busby's patched up team were vastly outclassed. Even more formidable than the pre-Munich team, the Spaniards lit up Old Trafford with an irresistible concoction of European and South American artistry and guile. None more than the irascible Magyar genius Ferenc Puskás. Rescued from footballing exile by Bernabéu, Puskás' god-sent ability and personable character added immensely to Madrid's already perfect storm. Wise as he was talented, the Magyar played the role of loyal Lieutenant to Di Stefano to perfection, preferring to waltz gloriously in the shade of the all-consuming shadow of the great Blond Arrow.

Also arriving in Madrid to perform alongside the holy trio of Di Stefano, Gento and Puskás was that other huge summer signing, the deceptively languid but utterly brilliant Brazilian playmaker Didi. He was joined by fellow countryman Canario and the wickedly gifted Uruguayan defender Jose Santamaria, who was a marvellous footballer, blessed not just in his ability to play and begin Madrid attacks, but also in the finest tradition of Uruguayan stoppers, willing when necessary to commit atrocities in defence. Christened by my dad as the 'Dirtiest greatest defender he has ever seen!' With an emotional but deafening 63,000 crowd roaring them on, United started brightly and Bobby Charlton twice went close with thunderous strikes that Real goalkeeper Dominquez did well to save. Then, on seven minutes, as if annoyed that Charlton possessed the cheek to attempt such acts, the visitors opened the scoring. A delightful through pass by the dazzling Didi to Puskás caused gasps of awe from the terraces. The Hungarian maestro waited for Harry Gregg to commit himself then, with great audacity, slipped the ball beyond the big Irishmen into the net. It was all done with the ease of one blessed with genius. After a spell in the wilderness caused by the break-up of the magnificent Hungarian 'Magyars 'with the

Hungarian revolution, Ferenc Puskas had shed the excess pounds, rolled back the years and was back!

It was soon 2-0 when on twenty-five minutes the scintillating, flashing pace of Francisco Gento set up Puskás who once more looked up and flashed a ridiculous, swerving drive past a flailing Gregg into the net. It was bewitching football. On the half hour it was 3-0: Real were relentless; with what appeared effortless skill Didi supplied a dagger of a pass into the path of an electric-heeled Alfredo Di Stefano who, without slowing down took the ball in stride before beating a besieged Harry Gregg with ease. Yet the best was still to come when moments before the interval Di Stefano delivered a moment of wizardry that bamboozled the United defence and made many in Old Trafford believe they were witnessing something quite unworldly.

Standing by a goalpost, he produced an outrageous back heel after trapping the ball with his heel before turning and flicking it past a befuddled Gregg.

At 4-0 Madrid left the pitch to huge applause from a home crowd that watched through disbelieving eyes their beauty and majesty. The breathtaking images of those gleaming white figures under the Old Trafford floodlights re-ignited memories of heroes lost. None more than Di Stefano whose magical piece of artistry for Real's fourth goal earned him a moving reception as he vacated the stage from an adoring, if still silently grieving audience.

United came out for the second half determined to save face; Albert Scanlon went close before Bobby Charlton sliced apart the Real Madrid defence allowing winger Warren Bradley to run through from the halfway line and score from a tight angle. Maybe a consolation only, but for Bradley, loaned to Manchester United by famed amateurs Bishop Auckland as they strove to regain their feet after Munich, it was a special moment. Warren Bradley's bravura effort served only to irritate the Spaniards and Real swiftly moved back into top gear.

The ball was passed with a tenderness and technique but kept from United's grasp like a child clutching his favourite toy. On sixty-three minutes a grateful Puskás accepted Didi's delightful pass before crossing for the unmarked Pepillo to make it 5-1 from close range. Pepillo had signed that same summer from Sevilla and was yet another Madrileño superstar in the making. As for Didi, this night, under the hazy glare of the Old Trafford floodlights was arguably his finest hour during a short and turbulent career in Madrid.

Twelve minutes from time and with United being dangled, toyed and prodded Francisco Gento suddenly got bored and exploded past a bedraggled United defence before almost breaking the back of the net with a ferocious finish past a desolate Harry Gregg. Beaten six times and at fault for none, Gregg was thoroughly fed up and cut a disconsolate figure.

Come full time and Real Madrid gathered in the centre-circle to take the acclaim of an adoring Mancunian public. Even the United players stayed behind to applaud the Madrileños off the pitch. It had quite simply proved a mis-match. Dennis Viollet spoke to the Manchester Evening News afterwards, "It seems an odd thing to say after losing 6-1 but I have to say I enjoyed that! They were special."

Munich had decimated Manchester United and a long time would pass before they could resemble a team good enough to give the European champions a real challenge. After the match Matt Busby was brutally honest in his summing up. "They have walloped us 6-1 and in doing so confirmed what I already know, that we have a long, long way to go to close the gap."

The newspaper headlines next day extolled Real Madrid's bravura showing.

THE DAILY HERALD: **REAL GIVE GREATEST SHOW ON EARTH!**

NEWS CHRONICLE: **SHOOTING SENORS SMACK IN SIX!**

DAILY MIRROR: **REAL PERFECTION!**

Whilst in Manchester, in a gesture so typical of the man, President Bernabéu took the entire Madrid party to visit Eddie Colman's grave at Weaste cemetery in Salford. There they stood, prayed and laid flowers. It was a touching moment for all. Salford and Archie Street where Eddie lived was half a world away from Madrid, but here they were. Paying tribute to the young lad from across the Trafford swing bridge they nicknamed 'Snakehips.'

Two days later a touch of Di Stefano and Puskás must have rubbed off on Manchester United as 41,000 returned to Old Trafford to witness the Red Devils thrash Leicester City 4-1. Charlton's opener on five minutes was followed by Viollet (2) and another from Quixall. The grim realities of this post-Munich, though ever present, were for once temporarily put aside for ninety minutes as United on an Old Trafford pitch still sprinkled with Madrileño gold dust sent supporters home smiling. That itself a small miracle in such trying times.

GAME 2

Wednesday, 11th November 1959. Six weeks on from the 6-1 massacre at Old Trafford, a return match was staged in Madrid with Manchester United and Matt Busby given the red-carpet treatment by Santiago Bernabéu from the moment they landed till the moment of their departure. A pleasant stay was tinged with real sadness at memories of events only two and a half years before when the Babes arrived so full of life and were adored by the Madrid public. Christened 'Los Chicos' by the Madrid newspapers they turned heads and captured hearts with their huge smiles, dashing suits and American type trilbies! Now, sadly, these same faces found only on faded black and white photographs.

United went to Spain on the back of a 3-3 draw away to Fulham in which a late Bobby Charlton goal salvaged a draw. Lying in sixth place their league form remained patchy and infuriating. A bookie's dream and a pundit's nightmare.
However, on their better days which could never be predicted, they remained a match for any team in England. A fact soon to be confirmed with events in the Bernabéu.
The affection and admiration for Manchester United was obvious amongst the Madrileño faithful as they handed the visitors a stirring welcome on entering the Bernabéu.
These new strangers in red shirts.
 As for the game, it turned out to be a remarkable match with United scaring the living daylights out of Real before finally going down in a 6-5 shootout! It was Boy's Own football.
An 80,000-crowd watched on in astonishment at the Estadio Bernabéu as the visitors raced into a shock two goal lead after only fifteen minutes. The first a penalty on twelve minutes after Bobby Charlton was cynically chopped down by Jose Santamaria, a man who clearly did not believe in friendlies and was in typical ferocious 'They shall not pass' mood. The goalkeeper Dominquez saved the initial shot from Albert Quixall, only to lie

helpless as the United man got lucky and lashed home the rebound. 0-1!

Quixall had been signed by Matt Busby to help rebuild his fallen empire in September 1958, from Sheffield Wednesday for a record fee of £45,000. The so called ''Golden boy," twenty-five-year-old cost £10,000 more than the previous highest transfer. His time up to that point had been disappointing at Old Trafford. Although rated highly, Quixall struggled to live up to the huge sum spent on him. United had become a place where you either thrived or died on the pressures of the shirt you wore and its one-time owner.

The fee for both sides was important though but for vastly different reasoning. Busby would later admit, "I was determined to keep the name of Manchester United on people's lips. We always had to look as if we were doing something. Having been the greatest we could not settle for anything less. Quixall was part of that."

As for Sheffield, their General manager Ernie Taylor was alleged to have said of the Quixall fee, "The real price was £25,000. The other £20,000 was for Mark Jones and David Pegg." Both Yorkshire schoolboys whom Wednesday had expected to have a career at Hillsborough and not Old Trafford, where fate's cruel hand clipped their wings far too early. The feelings across the Pennines cut deep with those two lads.

Sixty seconds later Albert Scanlon skipped clear of Marquitos and his long searching pass was picked up by Warren Bradley. Racing past the defender Pachin, Bradley let fly and his shot deflected off Santamaria and beat Dominguez to silence the stadium. The Madrid crowd were shocked and they soon let their heroes know about it.

However, at the opposite end they had no quarrels warmly applauding Harry Gregg, who after his nightmare experience at Real's hands in Manchester was busy banishing ghosts. Two sensational saves by the big Irishman as the Spaniards turned up the heat from Enrique Mateos and Alfredo Di Stefano brought the Bernabéu to it's feet, as Gregg staged a one man show of defiance. He was finally beaten on twenty-one minutes but only by a debatable penalty after a very soft handball was alleged against Bill Foulkes. Up stepped Di Stefano to thrash the ball past Gregg and halve the deficit. Immediately, the crowd's spirits were raised and they shook life into a so far listless home side. Game on, but just when it was thought Madrid would switch into overdrive, United struck again. On the half hour the reds broke out en masse and a four man move between Freddie Goodwin, Albert Scanlon, Bobby Charlton and Dennis Viollet saw the latter sweep the ball past Dominquez from five yards. It was football

Madrileños style by the boys from Manchester! A feeling of bemusement filled the stadium for though classed only as a friendly, it was thought unthinkable for Real Madrid to be 3-1 down on home soil? The natives were restless. This wasn't how things went down in the Bernabéu.

Gregg's heroics in the United goal hardly helped their mood as he threw himself around in order to keep out a barrage of shots. However, good fortune favoured the Spaniards once more when moments before the interval a clearly offside Mateos was allowed to run through and score. At 3-2 they had been handed a lifeline. It was cruel on the Mancunians whom knew they now faced a second half onslaught from the European champions.

Five minutes after the break normal service appeared to have been resumed as Real drew level. A brilliant through ball was latched onto by their latest wonder kid, nineteen-year old Seville born Manuel Bueno, who fired the equaliser past a diving Harry Gregg. A frustrated Gregg pounded the turf in frustration at being beaten. Bueno was a truly outstanding talent but due to such riches of talent at the Bernabéu his appearances were limited. Now, the Madrileños turned up the gas. They pinned Manchester United back and hardly needed the helping hand of a clearly out of his depth French referee Monsieur Barberan who, on fifty-four minutes, produced another shocking decision by awarding a penalty for an innocuous challenge by Goodwin on Mateos.

This proved the last straw for the visitors whom blazed in anger at the inept official. Friendly or not Barbcran's refereeing was verging on scandalous. Step forward the 'Blond Arrow.' After having a quiet word with the United players, Alfredo Di Stefano appeared to gesture an apology to the crowd before purposely hammering his penalty over the bar.

There was class and then there was Di Stefano.

Two minutes later United edged back in front when winger Albert Scanlon released Bobby Charlton to crash a powerful shot in off the post past Dominguez. Charlton had been wonderful throughout and appeared comfortable playing on such a stage. He was turning heads in Madrid and was the subject of overt flattery from Madrid officials which included an unexpected encounter at Madrid airport with Don Raimondo Saporta. The charismatic fixer embraced the startled United player before asking, "So what do you think Bobby, would you like to come play in Madrid?"
Happily, for Manchester United supporters, Bobby Charlton politely turned down the offer. He had no ambition to ply his trade elsewhere and no amount of Spanish gold would tempt Charlton abroad. Madrid had its attraction; the money, the sun, playing alongside Di Stefano and Puskás every

week but it wasn't Old Trafford.

It wasn't home.

In the immediate aftermath of Munich, it was Charlton, still only twenty-years old and now without doubt the most talented of those still plying their trade at United who dragged them through the dark days. Though scarred from the loss of dear friends and forever to be haunted by his experiences in the crash, Charlton played like a man possessed in the red shirt.

The last half hour saw Real up their game significantly with Alfredo Di Stefano seemingly on a mission to make up for his deliberate penalty miss. The Blond Arrow proved unplayable, like a ghostly white wind he flitted across the pitch, impossible to mark and thrusting passes like swords through the United defence. Three times he shredded the thin red line and each was put away with aplomb past Gregg by the sensational Bueno. It was a superb twenty-minute hat trick that left the visitors reeling, Harry Gregg speechless and the match surely safe for the home side.

Out came the white handkerchiefs in tribute; a rare moment in the sun for Bueno who acknowledged the crowds chanting his name. But still United came back, refusing to lie down they scored again in the dying embers of the contest when substitute, Alec Dawson, cut in from the touchline and hit a scorching drive past Dominguez making it 6-5. The Mancunians simply wouldn't give up!

A classic encounter finally ended and despite being light years away from the Madrileños in terms of class, Busby's men had shown a spirit that boded well for the future. Come full time both teams were cheered to the rafters as the Bernabéu displayed their appreciation for a memorable spectacle.

That evening Santiago Bernabéu spoke at a money raising banquet organised by the Spaniards for the families of those killed at Munich. In a speech the Madrid President revealed once more of his huge respect for the United manager. He told the assembled guests, "Matt Busby is not only the bravest, but the greatest man I have ever met in football." Words spoken from the heart.

They would meet again.

MADRID. For one man, a Major without the stripes but a football God to countless thousands, the 1960 European cup final could not come around fast enough. For ten years his had been a football tale of epic scale. One rich in drama, laced with unbridled passion, tears and joy but, so far, without a single major trophy. On 18th May 1960, the opportunity would finally arise to end such an undeserved famine. For Real Madrid, victory over Eintracht Frankfurt would signal a fifth consecutive triumph, another notch on a gloriously unfolding dynasty. The Madrileños prepared to unveil the curtain and present for eternity - an abiding monument. They were the white angels without wings weaving a masterpiece.

They were Real Madrid.

Now fast approaching his thirty-fourth year, the sands of time were shifting quickly for Ferenc Puskás. Like lightning striking through the night sky the 'Galloping Major' had illuminated the European game for a decade. Surely in Glasgow he would finally receive due reward? However, there was drama in the lead up to the final when it appeared Real's opponents were set to pull out of the competition.

An incident years before in the bitter aftermath of the 1954 World cup final had returned to haunt him when a raging Ferenc Puskás had claimed, after Hungary's incredulous defeat to Germany, that their opponents were, "Doped up to the eyeballs." He also told all whom would listen that he had witnessed "Needles on the German dressing room floor."

These serious allegations had never been forgotten by the German football authorities and they banned all their teams from playing clubs in which he featured. For years Ferenc Puskás had refused to back down. However, once the team had come through the semi-finals and it became known that

Real would be up against German opposition, Don Santiago Bernabéu acted. He persuaded the Hungarian to agree for his signature to be added to a letter of apology drafted by Raimondo Saporta. Whether Puskás actually signed it remains highly dubious but it was delivered personally to the Germans by Saporta who, with typical charm and grace, solved the problem and thoughts turned back to football.

There were journalists and footballing realists who proclaimed loudly beforehand that events at Hampden Park could well be Puskás' and perhaps more so Alfredo Di Stefano's swansong. The 'Blond Arrow' was approaching his mid-thirties and though showing no signs of waning, human frailties affected legends also - though none dared ever suggest such to Di Stefano's face.

The city of Glasgow found itself torn in two on whom to support. The Protestant supporters of Rangers were firmly behind the Germans, whilst Celtic's Catholics formed in procession behind the pride of the Spanish church. Sadly, when it came to the putrid question of Sectarianism, Glasgow society remained stricken more than most. It was shameful that a sporting occasion as the European cup final should have been dragged down to such ridiculous divides. Luckily, Real Madrid were set to show that football, Madrileño style crosses all borders, no matter how dark or bigoted. For on a gentle, warm Scottish evening 127,000 would gather to witness football from heaven. Glasgow was set for not just a football, but a religious enlightenment by what was soon to unfold in their great city.

Real's opponents were arguably their toughest opponents in a final to date. A crack German outfit bristling with pace and skill, they were doggedly resistant and technically astute. Eintracht had all but obliterated Glasgow Rangers over both legs of the semi-final. The Scottish champions were totally unaware of their little-known opponent's qualities when they had arrived in Germany, to such an extent that Rangers manager Scott Symon declared he had never heard of them? It proved a regrettable comment when the Scots found themselves totally outclassed and thrashed 6-1 in Frankfurt. Then, there was the further red-faced embarrassment at Ibrox where they were torn apart 6-3. By this time Symon knew them well and had seen more than enough of the Germans.

Eintracht travelled to Glasgow for a second time feared, respected and threatening to hand Real Madrid a most severe examination of their legendary status. The Germans began in the same form that demolished Rangers. Playing fast, incisive and utterly gripping football, they broke quickly down both flanks and rocked Madrid early on. Their left-winger Eric Meier smashing a shot violently against the Real crossbar from close range in the opening minutes.

The shock reverberated across Hampden as the reality dawned on all present that the Madrileños had a real game on their hands.

Real hit back. The latest superstar, twenty-five-year-old Luis Del Sol, had signed the previous January from Betis for six million Pesetas and was a darting left-sided winger with gazelle like pace and swift balletic feet to match. He brought the Eintracht goalkeeper Egon Loy to his knees with a low shot to signal that Real had awoke.

Yet still the Germans swarmed forward and twenty minutes in Hampden was in rapture when they took a deserved lead. A superb cross from Eintracht's centre-forward Erwin Stein was missed by Jose Santamaria and landed at the feet of experienced right-winger Richard Kreis, who slammed a fierce shot at the near post past a dumbfounded Dominguez.

Madrid appeared stunned and an irate Di Stefano handed Santamaria an aristocratic mouthful for allowing Stein to escape his shackles.

As if Madrileño pride had been pricked by the temerity of going behind, the white shirts suddenly switched gears; their football became typically whiplash, deadly and cajoling. Six minutes later the Brazilian Canario careered downfield and crossed for the 'Blond Arrow' to steer an equaliser past

Loy. Di Stefano had now scored in every European final played so far, it was a stunning record from a player who along with his compadres was set to inflict wanton devastation on the unsuspecting Germans.

Eintracht were pushed back, overpowered and unable to get near the ball. On thirty minutes the incessant pressure on the Frankfurt rearguard told when a nervous Loy fumbled, allowing a quick thinking Di Stefano to swoop making it 2-1. The Germans found themselves in a strange world. Treated like stooges on a conjurer's stage.

With a nonchalance born of the fact they were good enough to do what they wanted, the Real players began to strut and stroll in possession. They had that whiff of blood, German red. Eintracht were a proud side, reduced to chasing after teasing Madrileños like a dog chasing a newspaper caught in a fierce wind. It was the beginning of the greatest footballing show on earth.

Time and again Francisco Gento, Del Sol and Canario ripped like dervishes past alarmed defenders to feed the lurking Ferenc Puskás. The Hungarian joined the carnival right on the interval when he let fly a thunderous strike from an impossible angle that somehow roared past Loy to secure a fifth trophy for Real.

At witnessing such an audacious strike, the Glasgow audience applauded this tubby little figure laced with awesome talent and possessing sticks of dynamite in his left foot. The second half saw little respite for Frankfurt as nine minutes in they were 4-1 down. The electric pace of Gento took him past the flustered Eintracht stopper Lutz before finally being brought to earth by the shattered German in the penalty area. A little shimmy and Ferenc Puskás placed his shoot past Loy with tormenting ease. Embarrassed, humiliated and crestfallen they may have been but the Germans refused to throw in the towel and instead fought on.

Meanwhile, Madrid showed off, they teased their opponents. Cruel but beautiful; the ball was stroked amongst the Madrileños with a rare forte of bewildering flicks. All performed with an intent to hurt and grind Eintracht into the turf. On sixty minutes Gento flew clear of Lutz, who trailed in a weary if dogged pursuit of 'El Motorcycle.' Waiting for Gento's cross was an impatient Puskás who struck to complete his hat trick and Madrid's fifth. Instigated by he of the balding pate and strutting manner, the carnage continued. Ten minutes later Puskás had a fourth, his best of the evening when he killed the ball dead in the penalty area and lashed home a ferocious shot past a shell-shocked Egon Loy. It was the Major's defining moment on a Glasgow night full of footballing sorcery and brought a moving reaction from an astonished crowd, whom were struggling to believe it with their own eyes. Maybe the gallop had turned more into a trot but the Hungarian's star still shone bright.

On eighty minutes and showing huge defiance, Frankfurt regained a modicum of self-respect when they pulled back a goal and earned a standing ovation in doing so. Stein lowering the deficit if not the feeling of humiliation which had engulfed all whom shared Eintracht's colours. The time was almost upon Glasgow for a last cameo to crown a performance that would echo in eternity as the greatest ever by any team. Enter stage right the 'Blond Arrow' to deliver a *coup de grace* and seal this bloody if magnificent slaughter. Playing any number of intricate passes in his own half, though only on the understanding he got the ball back, Di Stefano glided around and past Eintracht shirts, before letting fly on the edge of the German penalty area – it was a snapshot all that summed up arguably the finest footballer of all time. A lone klaxon roared out in Teutonic defiance across Hampden as fifteen minutes from time Eintracht pulled back another consolation. Stein earning himself a brace of goals and small satisfaction on a night when his team had been torn apart.

The final whistle was sounded by English referee Jack Mowatt with Alfredo Di Stefano and Ferenc Puskás competing to have the last touch so they could claim the match ball. The 'Major's' four and

'Blond Arrow's' three ending any semblance of argument that Real's finest remained untouchable. It was a show of strength unrivalled in the tournament's short history and a message to any whom dared to take their crown. As for the ball? Puskás won out, only to then hand it to a Frankfurt defender who pleaded with him for a memento. After the pain inflicted by he and his team, how could the Hungarian refuse? The Scottish spectators stood en masse to acclaim the Spanish masters as the BBC commentator that evening Kenneth Wolstenholme described their football as "Swan lake on turf." High regard was paid to the distraught Germans whom remained on the field and performed a guard of honour for the victors. Eintracht would return home well beaten and humbled but proud of the fact they had played a part, albeit unwillingly, in the greatest match of all time. A testament to a glorious era.

Real Madrid 7 Eintracht Frankfurt 3.

On the terraces many simply refused to leave, desperate to soak up the atmosphere and hold on to the sweet memories. Long after the Madrileños had bade a fond farewell from the centre-circle and disappeared into the dressing room, thousands of Glaswegians remained gazing out onto the pitch. The unforgettable scene of magic and wonder where Di Stefano and Puskás had run riot. The Spaniards were going nowhere as that night

Glasgow's huge heart belonged to them. The Scots celebrated as if the victory were their own. The next day saw the players paraded around the city on an open-topped bus, nursing giant sized hangovers. The result of all night partying with more than receptive hosts.

Finally, after a civic reception at Glasgow town hall where the European Cup trophy took pride of place, they retired to the relative sanctity of the airport. Though even there the party continued as thousands of Scots awaited to wish them well and a safe journey back to Madrid. As the plane soared off the runway taking the European champions home, the cheers of Glasgow still rang loud. In a city hardly rich in gold but the possessor of poets in abundance, and a love of the beautiful game to rival anywhere, 18th May 1960, entered local folklore; in a way Real Madrid never went home.

Finally, the Major Ferenc Puskás had a much-deserved medal to show for a glorious career and as the sixties dawned the Madrileños were quite literally on top of the world. A goodwill orgy towards Real ensued by all, except one, Barcelona: the Catalans not appreciative of the admiration and affection shown towards a football club they despised with a vengeance. It was time to curtail this love fest, for it had become clear the only team capable of ending the nightmare was FC Barcelona. A time of reckoning drew near between the warring clubs, one set to shake the foundations of European football.

Meanwhile,
UNITED. Manchester United were entrenched in a desperate struggle for survival; 1-0 down at Bolton Wanderers with just fifteen minutes remaining these were traumatic times for the Old Trafford club. The first three months of the season had proved horrific with only two games won and first division survival looking dubious. It was the worst start to a campaign for United since World War Two and the unspoken word was finally being uttered around the club. One since Munich few dared to mention - Relegation. As the Burnden Park hordes rejoiced in the misery of their famous big city neighbours, an eighteen-year-old Manchester United débutante called Norbert Stiles stepped forward to save the day...

A right-half and former altar boy from the United hotbed of North Manchester, Stiles set up his close friend and team-mate, Irish midfielder Johnny Giles to run on and finish superbly past Bolton goalkeeper Hopkinson. The Daily Express next day summing up United's relief. **STILES TO GILES: ALL SMILES!** A valuable point was earned by two boys brought through United's youth scheme to prove some things at Old Trafford never changed.

Five months on from their historic 7-3 victory over Eintracht Frankfurt at Hampden Park, Real Madrid again took on Manchester United in the latest in a series of friendlies that were starting to take on a life of their own. The relationship between the two clubs had grown to something quite extraordinary in Munich's shadow. A typical example came when it was thought Alfredo Di Stefano and Ferenc Puskás might not have been fit to travel, Santiago Bernabéu phoned Matt Busby, and asked if he wished to postpone the game until Real's leading lights were fit? However not wishing to appear ungrateful to the Madrileños Matt Busby insisted they come anyway.
Busby informed the Real President that "Real Madrid had become like family and whether bearing their most fabulous gifts or not Manchester was eagerly anticipating their visit." On hearing this Bernabéu relayed Busby's message to Di Stefano and Puskás, whom then decided to travel and if possible at least play some part of the game.

GAME 3

''You are playing with my money!'' Alfredo Di Stefano.
Wednesday, 13th October, 1960. With the 'Little Cannonball' and the 'Blond Arrow' as ever in the visitor's line up, 50,000 supporters welcomed back Real Madrid to Old Trafford. The dazzling sight of

those gleaming white shirts under floodlights was the stuff of dreams. Memories were still fresh of the Madrileños in their absolute pomp ripping apart the unfortunate Germans at Hampden Park. Many on the terrace feared total carnage if Madrid were in similar mood and after just nineteen minutes a delightful pass from Puskás found Di Stefano who slammed a wonderful shot past Harry Gregg. Old Trafford held its collective breath then warmly applauded. Lancashire's ground sat only within short walking ground of the football stadium and with a cricket score looking set for the evening a wag in the crowd joked maybe they should have played the game there!

Amid the spellbound masses that night who stood enraptured as the Madrileños performed their pre-match warm up routine was fifteen-year-old George Best. The Belfast boy had just arrived in Manchester and felt unable to take his eyes off Francisco Gento as he performed for an awe-struck audience. The Real goalkeeper Vicente dropped kicked the ball to a waiting Gento twenty yards away. 'El Motorcycle' dragged down the ball in mid-air with a magician's ease. Then, as if passing back to Vicente, Gento's intended hit suddenly stopped on contact with the ground and spun back towards him. Gasps fall down from the terraces, as Francisco took a bow. Applause broke out. The greatest footballing show on earth was once again set to descend on Old Trafford.

Like rain falling in Manchester, a goal for Alfredo Di Stefano against United was equally expected and it came early. Real appeared in troublesome mood as the ball was moved waspishly across the field. There did however, not appear the intent to twist the dagger any deeper into the hospitable Mancunians, the visitors had come to put on a show, display a few tricks and go home. Di Stefano could sense this and began to lose his imperial temper with strutting team mates. He feared complacency.

United began to make their own opportunities; Bobby Charlton, who always impressed against the Spaniards, let fly only for Vicente to leap magnificently and tip over the bar. Roused by Charlton's effort the noise level soared and on thirty minutes to the utter disgust of Di Stefano the home side equalised. A Charlton in-swinging corner was headed clear by Jose Santamaria, only for Albert Quixall to launch it back into the penalty area. As Vicente came to meet the ball a quick-thinking Mark Pearson reacted first to flick from six yards past him into the net. 1-1!

Pearson was a big favourite of Jimmy Murphy's; an inside forward, small but tough and brimming with talent. He had been thrust into the reserves to carry the flag after Munich and made his début like so many on that tear-stained night against Sheffield

Wednesday. Now, Mark Pearson had rocked the European champions.

Suddenly, it was all United as Real Madrid, seemingly stuck in showboat mode were forced back. Again, Bobby Charlton cut a swathe past chasing white shirts before flashing a shot inches wide and into the side netting. By this time the 'Blond Arrow' was apoplectic with rage! Reacting and probably a little fearful for what awaited them in the half time interval, the Madrileños upped gears. Ferenc Puskás, who had walked around uninterested for the previous thirty-eight minutes, revived to leave three players on their backsides, before laying off a pass for Jose Maria Vidal to hammer from twenty-five yards past Harry Gregg into the goal. As the half-time whistle was set to blow a now focused Puskás lashed in a ferocious left footed shot that Gregg did well to see never mind save – it was a timely reminder that inside the squat looking number ten with the oily greased hair lurked one of the all-time greats.

Alfredo Di Stefano wasted no time venting his spleen as he began tearing a strip off a shocked Ferenc Puskás even before they had reached the privacy of the Old Trafford tunnel. A public dressing down was not appreciated by the Hungarian who appeared to just shrug his shoulders at the Argentine, as if to suggest, "It is just a friendly Alfredo. Why are you getting so wound up?" But an irate Di Stefano was not for softening and the accusing finger pointed at Puskás was because he knew that Real Madrid could never afford to let down their guard. The same effort must apply in every game, be it a meaningless friendly or European cup final. The path to ruin lay in complacency, and Di Stefano was not about to let such happen.

Watching on fascinated was United youngster Nobby Stiles who could not believe what he was witnessing, as two of the greatest players in the world almost came to blows with so little at stake. But for Stiles it was an important lesson, one he would learn well. For fate had decreed a magnificent career for this unlikely looking hero, a short-sighted youngster from the Saint Patrick's congregation on Livesey Street who, on the day of the crash had raced home from the ground and into the church where he prayed desperately for the lives of his idols. To let them all return safe, especially Eddie Colman. Only then to be left desolate as Manchester faced the grim realisation that most, including Colman had been killed.

Now, as he watched Alfredo Di Stefano, the integrity of such a man to give his best all the time and insist others did similar. Nobby Stiles realised just what separated the mortals from the great Argentine. The heated debate continued on in the Real dressing room as Di Stefano turned his considerable wrath on others he deemed not performing to the expected standards. Through the walls shouting could be heard, with one voice above all. Any cynics in the vicinity whom ever doubted Real Madrid's professionalism and ambition to treat these matches as ultra-serious affairs would have changed their opinion as Di Stefano was heard yelling and demanding more from his under-performing compadres. None dared disagree, others preferred to say nothing and just hope Alfredo's temper would blow itself out if the game was won and that the £60-win bonus offer would help soothe matters. Even as the Madrileño's re-entered the field arguments were still raging with a visibly fed up Puskás still on the receiving end of a Di Stefano's tongue lashing.

The second half saw a Real Madrid team with their ears still ringing, intent on proving a point to a certain Argentine. Francisco Gento, a particular target, left defender Shay Brennan in a heap before being stopped at the last by the long legs of Bill Foulkes. Brennan's brave attempt to halt Gento as he sprinted clear left him unable to carry on and making his début, eighteen-year old Irish full back Tony Dunne replaced him, another like Stiles destined for glory in a red shirt.

As Madrid looked for a third to kill off United, a defence which had been pilloried all season somehow held firm. It was no longer a friendly as tackles flew and the game's competitive edge was evident by Real's Santamaria, whose challenges if committed off pitch would have seen him spending the night in a Manchester police cell. Followed by a longer spell in Strangeways. On seventy minutes a fierce, hard fought encounter was decided in the visitor's favour when the gazelle-like Brazilian Canario sprung to fire past Harry Gregg and seal the result. It could have been 4-1 moments later when Ferenc Puskás, now busy trying to ram Di Stefano's words back down his throat, laid on Gento, whose first time cross found the 'Blond Arrow', only for his goal bound shot to be blocked by substitute Tony Dunne on the goal-line, much to the Argentine's chagrin.

To Manchester United's credit they kept going and despite a series of further Real opportunities, all wastefully scorned, two minutes from time they grabbed a deserved second. Bobby Charlton, forever involved as he ripped dangerously down the wing, crossed dangerously, only for a Madrid defender to head clear. The ball fell thirty yards out at the feet of twenty-one-year-old Belfast born midfielder, Jimmy Nicholson. Looking up the Irishman picked his spot and thundered a stunning effort into Vicente's top left-hand corner. It was a goal that electrified Old Trafford and a fitting finale to what had been yet another fascinating clash between two football clubs still seemingly heading in separate directions.

However, this had been by far United's best performance of the season. The final whistle saw the home players form a guard of honour and applaud the Madrileño's off stage. Though not before Di Stefano and his compadres, all friends again, bade "Adiós" from the centre-circle to a crowd they never tired of delighting.

Once more, under the Mancunian stars, it had been a special night. It was unfair maybe to measure United's progress since the crash against such vaunted opponents, but ever so slowly, despite their league showing, Matt Busby felt they were coming back to life. He appreciated more signings would be needed, fresh blood to go alongside the likes of Bobby Charlton, Nobby Stiles and Tony Dunne and though not blessed in being able to see into the future, Busby, for the first time since Munich sensed hope as the battle to restore his ravaged club continued unabated.

The following Saturday United returned to league action at champions Burnley and despite a Dennis Viollet hat trick went down 6-3. It was a dreadful result which left them second from bottom and facing an uphill task to survive in a hellish season. United had not been out of the last four all season and with the referee that day a certain Mr Hemingway, it appeared the bell was tolling for an ailing football club.

MADRID. It was 6th August 1936. A blazing red sun set low over the Guadamarra mountain peaks in Northern Spain, as FC Barcelona president Josep Sunyol was led out into a Nationalist army courtyard. Condemned to death by firing squad, a blindfold was placed over Sunyol's eyes as a priest administered the last rites. The President awaited his fate with courage and seconds later militia loyal to Franco took aim and shot him dead. Sunyol's crime had been to drive accidentally into Fascist territory, and when his identity was made known the sentence was a hail of bullets through his Catalan heart...

Twenty-four years, 3 months and 19 days later came the momentous events of 25th November 1960, when the memory of President Sunyol could be suitably honoured with revenge for his execution as all Catalonia rejoiced in knocking Real Madrid off their European perch. Press wires across the continent blazed and few could believe it was really all over. Only six months on from the Masterpiece in Glasgow the Madrileño's reign was brought to an abrupt end. The Bernabéu walls had been breached by their most ferocious enemy and in Barcelona the fireworks erupted and the celebrations began.

Following Helenio Herrera's traumatic departure the previous season and after being beaten, humiliated by Real at the semi-final stage, Barca had recovered sufficiently to hang on to their league title by the slightest of margins. Thus, gaining entry back into the European cup and another opportunity for revenge. Herrera's replacement was the veteran Yugoslav coach Ljubisa Brocic. A former Juventus and PSV Eindhoven coach, he had arrived in Catalonia with a fine reputation, which was further enhanced amongst the Barca supporters when he managed to prise away the great central defender Jesus Garay from Athletico Bilbao. A serious and thoughtful man, Brocic had but one agenda - to rid the Catalans of the eternal stone in their shoe called Real Madrid. Immortality beckoned early on in his Nou Comp career when fate intervened to ensure Barca were sensationally drawn to play the European champions in just the second round. As all Spain held its breath the opportunity arose for Ljubisa Brocic to finish off a legend and earn for himself a place in Catalan folklore.

The animosity between the two clubs did not always extend to the players. Especially the foreign contingents and the Hungarians in particular. Having shared so much before, fellow Magyars Ferenc Puskás together with Zoltan Czibor and Sandor Kocsis maintained a close friendship. Whenever the teams played in Barcelona the three would quietly arrange a meeting where they would talk of times gone by, toast old comrades – these were men whom had witnessed their own nation erupt into fire and flames, who had lost close friends and family in a doomed uprising and were not about to fall out over somebody else's war. The rampant hostility which existed between Catalonia and Castille showed itself in many forms and on this occasion the Magyars felt unable to meet up when the two clashed in the Spanish capital. They daren't risk it. For in an atmosphere teeming with the rancid odour of the civil war, the visitors never hung around long in Madrid to swap handshakes, never mind pleasantries and drinks. Here, General Franco, the devil on earth for all Catalans, still resided and the horrific memories of Stukas dive bombing, screaming low over Barcelona and slaughtering innocent civilians remained fresh in minds. Their officials were never prepared, unless left with no option, to break bread in President Santiago Bernabéu's hospitality suite. And yet, even amid such hatred the Hungarian trio's relationship remained strong. Until the fateful European cup draw in which they were paired together for the second time, then the laughing stopped, as even they realised the consequences of defeat. The controversial events of the two forthcoming matches would test their bond of unity to its extreme. For it was a war, maybe only on a football pitch but war nonetheless and one had to take sides.

Madrid hosted the first-leg and, as was their wont, FC Barcelona arrived at the latest possible hour - they were hardly keen on sight-seeing. Come kick off on 9th November 1960, the Estadio Bernabéu was awash with tension and excitement. A spectacular sea of white flags coveted the stadium. Fireworks crashed, flares whizzed and flew. Rockets shot high into the Madrid sky. The noise from a nervous but expectant crowd utterly deafening. 100,000 demanding Catalan blood. They did not have long to wait for in the opening minutes Enrique Mateos swooped to hand Real a dream start. Stirred by Mateos' opener Real went for an early kill, but despite close shaves Barca survived. Then, against all odds, they struck an unlikely equaliser on a rare foray over the halfway line. On thirty-minutes a Luis Suarez free kick deceived Vicente and soared into the net. A deathly silence descended on the Bernabéu, the celebrating Barca players saluted their bench as a hail of abuse fell upon their heads. Words were not deemed necessary to appreciate just what the goal meant to the Catalans.

The massacre expected by the home crowd after such a promising beginning failed to materialise and as the interval drew near Barca looked to have survived the worst excesses of Di Stefano, Puskás et al. As groans and whistles accompanied every misplaced Real pass the tension rose, only then for Francisco Gento on thirty-three minutes to latch onto a loose pass and fire his side back in front. It was so unexpected, but delighted this footballing cathedral. Gento's lightning finish looked to have restored confidence amongst home players and fans, handing new found belief to all of Madrileño persuasion that Barca would be finished off second half. But Real had not played well, their brightest stars struggled and appearing at all too human. Worrying.

As the contest wore on Real seemed content with a 2-1 lead and sought not to lose rather their gain further advantage. The Bernabéu terraces whistled with disdain, a support spoilt beyond all measure by success now turning on a team that had only ever brought untold glory. Two minutes from time came the sting in the proverbial tail when Barca midfielder Evaristo split the home defence and put Sandor Kocsis clear on goal. The Madrid defenders appealed desperately for offside and for a second were relieved when the linesman put up his flag. Only to watch aghast as the English referee Arthur Ellis refuted his assistant's claim and waved play on. On went Kocsis into the penalty area, only to be sent sprawling by Vicente. To the abject disgust of almost all in the Bernabéu, Ellis pointed to the spot. As the Madrileños surrounded both the referee and linesman Luis Suarez prepared for a defining moment in the history of both clubs. Mr Ellis had no intention of backing down and when the arguments calmed Suarez swept the penalty past Vicente to ignite wild scenes of joy in Catalonia and send Madrid into mourning. It finished 2-2 and for the first time Real Madrid had failed to win a home tie. The omens were foreboding, the mood dark as the champions vacated the arena to loud boos.

An irate Ferenc Puskás seethed over the last-minute drama and manhandled Kocsis, accusing him of diving. The strains of 'El Classico' finally breaking the chains of a Hungarian friendship. Puskás later recalled that his old friend, "Could not look him in the eye" and swiftly retreated into the safety of a joyful Barcelona dressing room. Those Madrid supporters present on that momentous evening all suspected one day the sword of defeat would fall upon their incredible run of success, but for it to be plunged into them by the demonic Catalan hordes? In just a fortnight's time the European champions would be going into the lion's den of the Nou Comp battling for their imperial lives.

It had been a bad night in Madrid.

Come the fateful night of 25th November 1960, and the Barca players delayed their entry onto the Nou Comp pitch, in order to allow their crowd full and unmitigated licence to unleash hell upon the heads of the visiting Madrileños. The abuse that rained down from the spiritual home of the Catalans came laced with the rancid memories of that proud region's recent history. Then, time came for the appearance of FC Barcelona and the volume of noise that followed could be heard far away as the mountains of Guadamarra.

Where ghosts of the past listened in and prayed for revenge.

It was to be another English referee, Reg Leafe, who was given the dubious honour of handling a game for which the saying "Football is war' 'could well have been written. Mr Leafe was to have the type of evening on which nightmares and conspiracy theories thrive. Yet, the truth was he was more likely hapless and inept than corrupt. The pressure and what was at stake for both sides simply too much for him to handle.

After an opening half hour that seethed with passion, but little flowing football, the deadlock was finally broken and again it was Sandor Kocsis who caused mayhem for the Madrid defence when his fiercely whipped in cross was deflected off Pachin into the net to leave Vicente stranded and on his knees in despair. Barca led for the first time on aggregate in four meetings. Twice, as Real rallied they had the ball in Barca's net, only to see both disallowed by the English referee. Surrounded by infuriated white shirts, Mr Leafe, like his countryman Arthur Ellis in the first-leg cared little for popularity contests and seemingly not for turning.

Half time came and went with the Catalans holding on grimly to their narrow lead. Knowing disaster loomed Real surged forward, Di Stefano smashed a ferocious low drive past Ramallets in the Barca goal, only for the ball to rebound off the post. It was all Madrid but the Barca defence was unyielding, a wall of red and blue. Puskás became frustrated, lashing out at the lack of service whilst the 'Blond Arrow' dropped ever deeper in sheer desperation to begin attacks. Never in their golden era had the Madrileños sailed so close to the wind. Disaster loomed. The Nou Comp raged and prayed as the white shirts surged forward in search of redemption. Nerves were shattered and all Catalonia was closer to hell than heaven at the thought that any moment a Madrileño would break their hearts.

Nine minutes from time Real Madrid were dead and buried.

A lightning counter attack by Barcelona caught the visitors with men short in defence. Away they sped on the break with the roar of the living and dead behind them. Finally, a cross into the Real box saw a leaping Evaristo direct a looping head past a frantic Vicente to surely end Madrid resistance? In a wild frenzy of madness, tears and undiluted joy the Nou Comp self-combusted! Across the pitch

Madrileños fell to their knees, exhausted and spent. Needing two goals just to stay alive all looked lost. Step forward Alfredo Di Stefano who stubbornly refused to accept the inevitable. The shaken knight roused for one last rally – a cavalry charge ensued as Real fought against the dying of the light. Two further goals were ruled out by Mr Leafe who appeared totally out of his depth in such an intimidating atmosphere. The Madrileños fumed, none more than Puskás who glared towards Leafe with what could only have been murderous intent. Told by Di Stefano to forget about the Englishman until after the game, the Hungarian appeared dumbfounded at Mr Leafe's 'strange' decisions.

Three minutes from time a chink of light appeared when to the Catalan's horror, Real grabbed a goal back. The Brazilian Canario stabbing the ball past Ramallets to set up a storming finale; Barca panicked, the weight of history choking them and their confidence falling away. Old self-doubts returned and Real Madrid went for their throats. Hanging on by the darn of a thread the unlikely defender Manuel Marquitos was handed the god given opportunity to level the tie, when with just Ramallets to beat from twelve-yards he shot inexplicably over the crossbar. The Real stopper dropped down in tears, for he knew. Even for a warrior like Marquitos it was hard to take.

With Di Stefano trying in vain to orchestrate one

more attack Mr Leafe blew to send all of Catalonia dancing in the streets and Madrid into a veil of tears. Trouble erupted post-match with Real players, notably Puskás and Di Stefano, confronting the referee before being hustled away. It would not end there as Reg Leafe and linesmen had later to be smuggled out of the Nou Comp, amid rumours of severe Madrileño retribution. Mr Leafe and his terrified colleagues were put into a waiting getaway car and driven by an English journalist into the safety of the Catalan night. They left behind a Madrid lynch mob searching the Nou Comp high and low to wring their necks in utter frustration. It was only the intervention of Don Santiago Bernabéu who calmed tempers and told his players to show some dignity in defeat that matters settled down.

When asked himself later that evening on what he thought of Leafe's "performance" Bernabéu declared with a straight poker face, "He was Barcelona's best player." Hardly a lover of Barca being a former Nationalist officer in the civil war, the Real President had infamously once claimed, "The only thing wrong with Catalonia is the Catalans." It was a comment not forgotten or ever forgiven in Barcelona. Along with his fallen team, Bernabéu returned to Madrid.

The Catalans were in dreamland. The spell had been broken and they felt it was almost their given right to go onto the final in Basle Switzerland and beat an emerging Benfica. An unhealthy over-confidence bordering on arrogance consumed Barca in the match. All that is except their two marvellous Hungarians, Zoltan Czibor and Sandor Kocsis. The venue of the Wankdorf stadium was where the Magyars lost in an unforgettable manner the 1954 final against the Germans. Both claimed to have dark premonitions beforehand. Their psyche permanently scarred by the torrid events of that summer, as were all Hungarians when they fell at the last. The Magyars' strange experience beforehand proved to be uncannily correct for despite Barcelona swamping the Portuguese for huge period of the final they went down rather unfairly 3-2.

Barca's presumptive claim to be heir apparent to a crown worn with such majesty by their bitter rivals proved an unwise boast. The realisation was they had to win, victory was more than essential, it was expected. "We must win or die" exclaimed General Manager Juan Gish. Ferocious competition with Madrid had left them mortgaged to the hilt on a new stadium on which it was said £1 million was still owed. To fulfil their finance payments Barca had been forced into an agreement to transfer one of their great stars, Luis Suarez, to Inter Milan for £160,000 after the final. Also, with the title going to Real Madrid, beating the Portuguese was their only guarantee of a place in the following year's competition as holders. And yet, on a beautiful Swiss evening, in the glorious shadow of the Alps, all went horribly wrong.

For two unforgivable errors by goalkeeper Anton Ramallets ultimately cost them dear. As the nightmare unfolded they struck the Benfica woodwork an astonishing six times and on the greatest night in their history fate conspired against them. Barca's Hungarian duo finished the final in floods of tears. Zoltan Czibor was inconsolable, lightning had struck them twice in the same place. The scant consolation for Czibor was that he scored one of the finest goals ever witnessed in a European final; a thundering thirty-yard rocket that hit the net with such a ferocity the Benfica goalkeeper could only stand and stare. On hearing of his countrymen's lament Ferenc Puskás could not help but raise a wry smile. "I heard they were on a huge bonus" he claimed. "Maybe that is what brought tears to their eyes?"

After the distress following their loss in the Nou Comp, Real had stormed back to life with a point to prove. Just weeks after their European exit at Barca's hands they returned to the scene of the crime and destroyed Barcelona 5-3 in a stunning performance. One man in particular was magnificent as Alfredo Di Stefano defied the many critics whom claimed he and his team were a busted flush after losing their European crown. Never more dangerous than with a point to prove, the 'Blond Arrow' wreaked mayhem on enemy territory. The loss of the European cup acted as severe motivation for the Madrileños and they stormed back to take the Spanish title off Barcelona and end the season as champions. Though no longer holders Real would take on Europe's elite once more. They wanted to show a doubting public the magic remained, that the candle still burned bright. Sadly, Di Stefano and Puskás would be up against an opponent whom even they would find impossible to overcome. Time.

The autumn leaves were falling.

GAME FOUR

Wednesday, 13th December 1961. For the first time since these two great clubs came together Real Madrid were no longer European champions. Defeat to Barcelona in the previous season's competition meant some cynics suggest their annual visit to Manchester, though still special, had lost just a smattering of glamour. Yet such thoughts disappeared as photographer's cameras clicked furiously to create a minor supernova of flashes around the tunnel area, momentarily blinding Spanish eyes, before the crowd's roar welcomed them onto the Old Trafford turf. Honouring a promise made in the wake of United's darkest days the Madrileños had returned to a city in which they remained footballing gods.

Coming into this match, Matt Busby's struggling team sat two places from the bottom of the first division. A disastrous run from early October had seen them incur terrible losses, such as 5-1 at Arsenal, consecutive 4-1 reverses against Ipswich and Burnley and a gruesome 5-1 slaughter by Everton. When they were five down at half time. United fell like a stone and early hopes for a decent campaign when they appeared settled in the top six became the bitter memories of a false dawn.

The normal full house which had accompanied every Real Madrid visit to Old Trafford was for once not forthcoming as only 43,000 turned up on a freezing December evening. Home crowds had dipped alarmingly as patience with their underperforming stars and those deemed simply not good enough to wear the red shirt finally snapped. Many stayed away also because they had little wish to see United treated like cannon fodder by the still reigning champions of Spain, if not the continent.

Real Madrid themselves were not in the finest of health. Age more than ailment troubled the Madrileños. Father Time was an enemy that even a side of their calibre could not overcome. And yet even with Puskás injured so not travelled, the likes of Di Stefano, Gento, Del Sol and Santamaria made the trip to Manchester, all four a class above any plying their trade at United, so the possibility of a rout remained.

Once again free from the stress of their first division survival battle, the United players relaxed and began against Real in menacing attacking form. With only fourteen minutes on the clock two United youngsters combined intelligently to beat the Real rearguard. The beguiling little schemer Johnny Giles setting up his team-mate, Manchester born inside-forward, nineteen-year old Phil Chisnall to race on and hammer past goalkeeper Araquistain. Chisnall was an astute passer of the ball with considerable natural talent who was viewed by Busy and Murphy as one with a chance. It was a rare chink of light for United supporters in a season that up until Chisnall's fine strike had drove them mad with frustration. Undeterred by this minor setback Real swiftly regrouped and laid siege to the home goal, but with a back four of Brennan, Dunne, Setters and Foulkes, United held their ground.

It couldn't last and three minutes before the interval Di Stefano from fully twenty-five yards picked his spot and crashed an unstoppable shot into the top corner that United reserve goalkeeper David Gaskell never saw to level. Di Stefano's customary goal on the Old Trafford turf proved a worthy addition to his glittering collection of strikes against the Mancunians. As he made his way back to the halfway line he was congratulated by his jubilant compadres, yet hardly a smile passed the Argentine's lips. For this was not so much a personal vendetta but something splendid for United supporters to remember him by. No hard feelings, simply ''Saludos dede Madrid!' ''Greetings from Madrid!''

Normally a moment such as this would signify a home collapse but instead it was United who came storming back. Three minutes into the second half a Jimmy Nicholson pass found recent signing from Arsenal, £35,000 Scottish International David Herd. Herd's United career began well before the goals dried up. Tormented by injury and lack of form the pent-up, twenty-seven-year-old Herd drove a clinical low shot past Araquistain to delight the home crowd and bring a little solace and light relief to his under-pressure manager Matt Busby. Immediately, on the ball hitting the net Real coach Miguel Munoz appeared to lose interest and substituted Alfredo Di Stefano, Francisco Gento and Jose Santamaria to save their ageing legs for more meaningful contests. Sensing a pivotal moment in the match the Old Trafford masses respected the three's departure from the pitch with a grand ovation, but then switched their attention to roaring their own side on to a morale-boosting victory.

The clock ticked on with both teams creating

chances. David Herd had what looked like a good effort ruled out for a foul, whilst Johnny Giles fired in a shot that beat Araquistain, but was cleared off the line by Pachin. Real struck back and inside forward Antonio Ruiz sneaked behind Shay Brennan before finishing with ease past Gaskell. Only to raise his hands in disbelief when called offside.

Then, with just ten minutes remaining, Herd scored a deserved second and United's third. Substitute Albert Quixall, who had replaced the injured Giles, split the Madrid defence and the forward gleefully lashed the ball past Araquistain's grasp. Game over and Old Trafford went wild! United rejoiced in the 3-1 scoreline – finally, at the seventh attempt, the spell had been broken. Though the Spaniards were clearly not the team of yesteryear, for Matt Busby and Jimmy Murphy, indeed all associated with Manchester United, it was a moment to cherish.

The final whistle bore witness to the fact that Real Madrid handled defeat with the same dignity and same class they treated victory

The Madrileños applauded both the crowd and United players before leaving the pitch to return home, and leave the stage clear for the victors to receive some much-deserved acclaim. Busby hoped the result would act as a spur for them to take into their league performances. Yet typically, the following Saturday disaster struck once more; a paltry 29,000 turned up at home expecting United to see off a West Ham side whom had not won there since 1935. An early goal from Herd looked to have set the Red Devils on the way to a convincing win, only for two late strikes from the Hammers gifting them the points. As a result, United remained only two places off the bottom of Division One and any good will earned in beating Real evaporated amid a chorus of boos across a half empty stadium. For Matt Busby, still in considerable pain from the crash, redemption had never felt so far away. Any thoughts of conquering Europe seemed now the talk of madmen. This United team on present form were going down.

MADRID. Like an aged movie queen who steadfastly refutes the onset of old age, so Real Madrid refused to go gently into the night, and in 1962 once more reached the European cup final. The Blond Arrow and the Major, both thirty-six years old, basked in the dying embers of an empire that was once thought invincible. Retirement was a notion that scared each into continued levels of performance defying both age and nature. Theirs's had been a wonderful partnership; Alfredo Di Stefano and Ferenc Puskás. Names etched forever in footballing folklore to be spoken of with awe. A lasting legacy that would stretch beyond the dimming pages of history books and one that both intended to crown with a last shot at glory...

However, these were changing times, it was in Lisbon and specifically Benfica's Estadio da Luz, where the banner of European champion now flew high and proud. Their nickname, the Eagles, was relevant to the height to which they had soared following their dramatic victory over Barcelona the previous season. As if the footballing gods were not handing out enough gifts to the Portuguese, they had in hiding a young colt who in time would come to be remembered and spoken of in the same hushed tones as Di Stefano and Puskás.

From the dirt strewn back alleys of a rat-infested shanty in Mozambique, the Black Panther sprung onto an unsuspecting world. Eusebio da Silva Ferreira was one of eight children raised by his widowed Mother. As a child he had played from dawn till dusk with brothers and a ball tied together by rags. As night fell he would stare upon the Mozambique sky with longing eyes and dream of escaping such a miserable existence. Never realising that already he had been selected to live his life a world away amongst the glittering stars. For the Eagles had come calling, Benfica awaited for this extraordinary young footballer.

His rise began as mere gossip in a Lisbon barbers shop. The Benfica coach Bela Guttman was being attended to in his favourite chair, happily relaxing when Carlos Bauer, an ex-player of Guttman's, now acting as a scout, came hurtling through the front door with the air of one who had just witnessed the second coming. A breathless Bauer stood staring at his boss before stating, "You are not going to believe what I have found for you."

Bauer told Guttman how he had just returned from a scouting trip to Mozambique and had unearthed a prodigy. "He is not of this world" the German exclaimed, "I swear he is not of this world." After hearing similar reports regarding the boy from others whose faith he trusted implicitly, plans were made to bring the young African to Lisbon.

But there was a problem.
Eusebio had already played junior football in Mozambique for one of Sporting Lisbon's junior teams. Sporting were Benfica's deadly city rivals and there was mutual hatred on both sides. Frankly, they detested each other's guts. Sporting were sure to resist Benfica's attempts to lure away their most precious asset. Word had already reached them of Bela Guttman's intent and plans were made to keep him at bay.
Unluckily for Sporting, they found themselves up against a wily old gypsy Jew whose plans to snare his prize would concentrate on the lair. Guttman met secretly with Eusebio's mother and offered her the princely amount of $20,000 for her special offspring's signature. Like any good son he did as

she insisted, for such a sum went a long way to putting food into the mouths of his brothers and sisters.

Benfica had their man, but this was only the first stage of Guttman's plan. Eusebio had now to be smuggled out of Mozambique and Sporting's sight. Already they had people at airports both in Portugal and Africa looking out for the player, and with orders to hold on tight to the Panther's reins. The dictat came down: do whatever it takes to prevent him wearing a Benfica shirt.

Always a step ahead, Bela Guttman had Eusebio disguised and discreetly boarding a plane to Lisbon. On landing he was whisked straight off the runway to a Benfica hideaway. All this whilst the Sporting welcome committee waited in the airport lobby wondering where on earth he had got to - they would soon realise and pay a heavy price for many years to follow.

Once Eusebio's kidnapping had been made legal, Benfica felt sufficiently confident to allow their new star to join his fellow Eagles in a training session. The sixty-two year old Bela Guttman could not believe his own eyes. He was said to have whispered on his first sighting up close of the teenage African.

"The boy is gold."

This was a man who had witnessed the best and worst of this world. Who had suffered and survived the horrors of a Nazi concentration camp. He was reduced to believing that after living through such terror, nothing could ever make his heart soar again. Guttman was wrong, for Eusebio had relit a spark in his soul. A footballer of limitless power and skill. Blessed with a Panther's spring and speed and lethal in front of goal. A true predator: Benfica could not believe their luck.

Like a punch-drunk boxer who cannot live without the sound of the bell and the smell of battle, so it was the Madrileños gathered in Amsterdam for what was being deemed a last stand. The path to their sixth European final had been dramatic as any before. A quarter-final clash against Juventus saw Real clinch a 1-0 win in Turin courtesy of Di Stefano. However, the game will be forever remembered by both sets of supporters for a clash between Juve's giant centre-forward John Charles and the visitor's Uruguayan henchman Jose Santamaria. It was a ferocious struggle that continued after the game in the tunnel. Only the timely intervention of Ferenc Puskás, who wrestled Santamaria away and quite literally threw him into the Madrid dressing room, ended the duel.

If the Spaniards thought the job complete, events in Madrid left them staggered as a lone strike from the diminutive Argentine maestro Omar Sivori silenced the Bernabéu and led to a Parisian play-off. Suddenly, at the final whistle, after being beaten for the first time on home soil, men such as Di Stefano and Puskás looked their age. Finally succumbing to the harsh realities of the rapidly advancing years, they looked ripe for the taking.

Still the swansong was put on hold as Real Madrid found they had enough left in their armoury to put Juventus away 3-1 in Paris. Sadly, it was a famous win tarnished by the on-going vendetta between Santamaria and Charles, who found himself victim of a Real defence that at times appeared intent on putting him in an early grave. The fine line between professionalism and butchery was crossed in sickening fashion as the financial incentives offered to Juve and Real players for success in this particular match meant they resorted to methods that shamed both clubs.

Goals from Luis Del Sol and Puskás saw Madrid through in the semi as they eased past Standard Liege. Benfica awaited in the final for this Madrid team whom simply refused to go quietly away. The old movie queen may have overdone the make-up to cover the wrinkles, but the Madrileños still had a puncher's shot of knocking out the reigning European champions.

Yet,

with Eusebio ready to be unleashed upon their waning legs few held hopes for a last miracle.

The seventh European cup final turned out to be

an enthralling match with a first-half performance from Real Madrid worthy of a glorious epitaph. For thirty-five minutes Di Stefano and Puskás rolled back the years. The Hungarian scored a remarkable hat-trick, all three laid on by the 'Blond Arrow.' It was astonishing football, Puskás scored the first with great poise after Di Stefano's deft, defence splitting-pass was hit with perfection. The second came from a drilled left-footed shot that screamed past Benfica goalkeeper Costa Pereira. Finally, the Major's crowning glory saw him side-step two Portuguese defenders before finishing with typical aplomb. But this was no one way romp, for in an outstanding opening, period Benfica scored twice themselves to keep Madrid in sight. Though out-played, Bela Guttmann's men had power, pace, flair and more importantly youth on their side.

Come the half time whistle, Puskás found himself mobbed as he left the pitch by the Real coaching staff. The Magyar looked weary, as did his compadres. Such a gallant effort had robbed them of much energy. Guttman watched this like a hawk eyeing its prey as the Madrid players trooped slowly down the tunnel.

In the dressing room he instructed his versatile all action midfielder Domciano Cavém to man-mark Di Stefano, he could no longer prowl at full speed the length of the pitch and had to content himself with sitting deep and launching attacks.

The Argentine may have had a battle plan in the head, but his legs would be unwilling and unable to carry it out. Cavém was told to stick tight and harass and deny the great man decent possession. Guttman's logic was sound – if you cut off the head, the body will fall and Real would be finished.

Eusebio had experienced a relatively quiet first period. Overawed at being so close to his boyhood idol Di Stefano, he struggled to find form. All that would change after a tongue-lashing from Guttmann who tore into his young prodigy.

'He is just human and an old man. You are Eusebio!'

With their talisman fired up the second half began with Benfica turning the screw and going hell for leather at the wilting Madrileños. The dazzling pace, movement and sheer tenacity of Eusebio, Augusto and Simões tortured the Real rearguard. Miserable through lack of service, Puskás dropped back to help out his beleaguered compadres, only to immediately lose possession as red shirts jumped upon him. Away went the towering Angolan midfielder Mario Coluna towards the Madrid goal. Coluna took aim from fully twenty-five yards and swept a skimming drive past Jose Araquistain. 3-3.

The Portuguese now swarmed all over the Spaniards. A distraught Di Stefano was close to despair as Cavém all but cut off his air supply, rendering him helpless as Real folded around him. The Madrid of yesteryear would have simply found another gear but not anymore. This was the endgame.

Eusebio was on fire, hurdling tackles, getting off shots, collecting the ball and running through a writhing masse of Spanish defenders. On sixty-five minutes Pachin erred and chopped down the unplayable 'Panther' in the penalty area as he streaked past him like a runaway train. Eusebio got up and dusted himself down before lashing his spot kick into the net.

Madrid heads dropped and they bore the look of a team resigned to defeat. There was to be no let off from Benfica, as urged on by Guttman, they went for a fifth killer goal. Three minutes after his penalty strike Eusebio robbed a flagging Santamaria and from just outside the box let fly to see his deflected effort inch past Araquistain, clinching a second successive European cup. At 5-3 it was all over and come the final whistle Benfica supporters raced in celebration onto the pitch to raise their heroes high. Amid the mayhem and wild scenes of jubilation, Di Stefano sought out Eusebio and embraced the young tormentor before handing him his shirt. It was a moment to cherish as the baton was passed, the old guard giving way to the new.

Real returned to Spain still refusing to believe it

was the end of the road. The fact that Benfica had ripped them to pieces at will in the second half appeared lost on the Madrileños. The doors of the Bernabéu doors had truly been blown open by the winds of change and the power base of European football now resided in Lisbon.

The aged movie queen had been unmasked,
the golden era of Real Madrid was truly over.

UNITED. In the aftermath of Real Madrid having their hearts ripped open by Benfica in the 1962 European cup final at the Olympic stadium in Amsterdam, Matt Busby was secretly meeting Torino's Mr Fix-it, the dapper Luigi "Gigi" Peronace. Their conversation centred around a young Scottish international centre-forward that was currently plying his electrifying talent in the Agnelli motor kingdom of Turin. The debonair, thirty-three-year-old Peronace specialised in the transfer of British players to and from Italy, Jimmy Greaves and John Charles being the two most notable. However, neither compared financially with what "Gigi" was set to secure for Manchester United. If they were willing to a pay a record transfer fee of £115,000, then Denis Law was theirs'.

Over a handshake the deal was done and the lawman was Old Trafford bound...

MADRID. These were sad times in Madrid, the dying days of a football empire. The barbarians were not so much at the gates, they had come roaring through and taken away what the Madrileños valued most, their cherished European crown. To rub salt into an already festering wound, Real had just been held 3-3 on home soil by Belgium champions Anderlecht in the first-round stage. The Belgians simply refusing to lie down and die in the Bernabéu as three times they hit back to cancel out Gento, Zoco and Di Stefano strikes. Among the visitors, was exciting twenty-year-old prospect Paul Van Himst, who terrorised the Madrid defence throughout. It was the beginning of a wonderful career for Van Himst, who in time became established as his nation 's greatest ever player.

They were left facing a hazardous second-leg in Brussels with the real possibility of being eliminated. No longer were there guarantees of them sailing amongst the stars, on a pedestal of one. For suddenly they had found themselves no better than mere mortals. With Di Stefano and Puskás now both the wrong side of thirty-six, it felt mad to even suggest another shot at the crown could be had without a massive transfusion of new blood. But whom in Madrid possessed sufficient heart or courage to tell these two living legends their time was over?

There were those ready to step up, a new breed of Madrileños. Amancio Amaro, Ramon Grosso, Pirri and Manuel Velásquez. All were being groomed to lead Real into the next golden age. However, in terms of sprinkling gold dust, technical excellence and sheer glamour, none could hold a candle to Di Stefano and Puskás, but their spirit, togetherness and never-say-die attitude meant that behind the scenes in the Bernabéu hopes were high for better days to return.

UNITED. To honour the thirteen-year career of Real Madrid stalwart Jose Maria Zarraga, Matt Busby took his Manchester United team to Spain, continuing a tradition borne out of tragedy, and one highly valued by both clubs. Despite the arrival of Denis Law, United were enduring a horrid start to their own league campaign. The previous season they had recovered sufficiently to finish a lowly fifteenth, when at one stage around Christmas they appeared certainties for the drop. Busby's acquisition of Law had seen hope abound in Manchester and the Scot began in sensational manner by scoring on his home début. Yet that goal became a high watermark in a disastrous run that by September's end and their arrival in Madrid, saw them languishing in sixteenth place. Four days earlier they had suffered the embarrassment of a home derby defeat to Manchester City, when even two goals from the former Maine Road favourite Law, proved insufficient to save an appalling day for the red half of Manchester. A crowd of 49,455 had watched in horror as blues new signing Alex Harley crashed home a winner with the game's last kick. United desperately needed a lift.

GAME FIVE

The match against Real Madrid would as on previous occasions, provide brief respite from domestic turmoil. A Madrid audience of 80,000 welcomed back Manchester United onto the sacred Bernabéu turf. Both line ups were shadows of their successful pasts, but the sheer imagery of Madrileño white and Mancunian red still captivated the Spanish public. It was a footballing romance that shown no signs of waning.

The game began in typical manner with Di Stefano now more selective in his choice of forward runs, but still dictating all aspects of the Real performance. Forever demanding the ball, pushing others into position, telling them where they should run, and finding team-mates with exquisite range of long and short passing. He was still an artist who retained a wondrous ability to paint beauty on the Bernabéu canvas, even if nowadays he was unable to complete it. Alfredo the great was getting old and it was killing him inside.

Following the 'Blond Arrow' wherever he strode

was United's Nobby Stiles. A constant irritant to the Argentine, the great man struggled to shake off Stiles' limpet like style. Niggling and harassing the Mancunian was no respecter of reputation on the pitch, but away from the action Nobby Stiles adored Alfredo Di Stefano. He had no bigger admirer. On it, Stiles, like his idol Eddie Colman seven years before, was driving Di Stefano to despair. On a torrid, sweltering evening in the Bernabéu, the Collyhurst boy was winning hands down. To such an extent that Madrid's famed number nine gave up the ghost and lost interest. With Di Stefano under lock and key, elsewhere Denis Law was causing gasps of wonder from a Bernabéu crowd that were normally reserved for their own. Law was at his simmering best, playing on the edge and willing to start a fight or finish a move. Prowling; his slim figure moved into scoring mode as if electrified. Law was a flashing red streak that tormented Real defenders. A predator the likes of which they had hardly faced.

The interval came with no score but the visitors much in the ascendancy. As the second half began the crowd became increasingly impatient at their team's lack of incoherency. Looking to spark some life and urgency Miguel Munoz brought on four substitutes, only then to find himself a goal down moments later.

Mark Pearson picked up a loose pass on the edge of

the Real penalty area and hit a first time left-footed snapshot that Vicente failed to hold. As the groans from the terraces poured down, the ball bobbled under the goalkeeper's body and into the net. Real supporters screamed abuse at the forlorn Vicente. These were changing times in Madrid.

The incredibly hostile home crowd resembled a baying-howling mob. Incredibly spoilt and incapable of handling what these present Madrileños were serving up they were reduced to silence with a masterly second United goal. Again, it was the explosive Law who proved impossible for the opposition to handle - the Scot split two home defenders with a deft pass to the feet of Johnny Giles. The little Dubliner had lit up this grand arena all night with his touch and guile. With space and time Giles crossed to perfection for David Herd, whose powerful header slammed into the top right-hand corner of Vicente's goal. From that moment people began leaving the stadium in droves. Those left behind stayed only to shout abuse at the unfortunate players they felt were white shirted impostors. The final whistle brought a polite ripple of applause across the stadium for United's fine showing.

The managers shook hands, not knowing that the next time they clashed would be for a place in the 1968 European cup final in which Manchester United would ultimately triumph. Since Munich, the clubs had grown increasingly close off the pitch and now, significantly, on it there was little to separate them. It was a true friendship, when most of their domestic rivals had seemed content to let United suffer, Real Madrid had shown themselves true champions of honour.

For Matt Busby any faint hopes that Manchester United's breath-taking *Bernabéu* display would help ignite their league performances was shot down in flames four days later when they faced Burnley at Old Trafford. The same line-up that so excelled in Madrid were mercilessly ravaged 5-2 by their Lancashire neighbours. Those two results were typical of one of United's most dramatic seasons. A battle against relegation ensued and supporters faced a rollercoaster of emotions that left them exhausted by season's end.

Yet just as the dogfight depressed the faithful, so an unexpected FA Cup run provided joy unconfined. By the end of it United fans sensed that the dark clouds enveloping Old Trafford for an eternity would shortly lift, and if not redemption, a welcoming ray of sunshine was set to warm the hearts of all associated with Manchester United football club.

UNITED. Since Munich, Old Trafford behind closed doors had become a turbulent and at times poisonous place to ply your trade. With Matt Busby suffering physically and mentally following the crash, he was incapable of exerting the same authority that once held power over everything that moved at the club. To make matters worse, Busby's decision making in the transfer market had become erratic. Between 1953 and 1957 there hadn't been a need to buy one single player but needs must and in he went. United desperately required new blood and some arrived whom in normal circumstances would not have been allowed a space in the Old Trafford car park, never mind the chance to pull on the sacred red shirt. With little time to double-check character, these existed only as a human life support machine for a club until better could be found.

The atmosphere was horrific, cliques formed, money a burning issue, there was never enough. The players remained on pauper's wages even after the maximum wage was lifted in 1961. For Busby it was all about the club. Manchester United came above everything. This meant the constant whiff of rebellion was a rotten fragrance felt by all. The old ways remained but were laughed and scoffed at. Sadly, for the new recruits of good stock, they were joining a troubled club. A wretched world where red ghosts haunted every corner of The Cliff training ground and the Old Trafford dressing room. The frequent Mancunian downpours hinted at a city still in grief. A flood of tears: lost voices echoed down every corridor, the players forever compared with the illustrious departed. Many of those chosen to followed in such hallowed footsteps neither cared or were good enough. In short United was a mess and going nowhere but down.

The survivors fared little better. There were strained relationships in the wake of Munich. No longer brothers-in-arms, a loathing developed amid the fortunate few with claims that Bill Foulkes for one *"ran away"* instead of trying to help their trapped, injured and dying team-mates. Harry Gregg and Bill Foulkes hated each other's guts, *"You should have seen that big bastard run"* the Irishman joked.

Where there were once shiny apples, now there were so many rotten eggs and it only took one to cause a stench. Established training methods were mocked: in November 1960 Busby splashed out £29,500 for West Ham's cultured, left sided defender, twenty-eight-year-old Noel Cantwell. Behind his manager's face Cantwell was incandescent with rage at what he felt was a shambolic amateur set-up. Cantwell had come from the self-styled West Ham Academy, a band of players whom had begun to think deeply about the game. Malcolm Allison, John Bond and Bobby Moore would gather after training in an Italian café around the corner from Upton Park and dissect the supposed merits of English football. How things had to change and adapt or be left behind. None were more vocal than Cantwell. Moving salt and pepper pots across the table to make a point the group exposed the myth of the long ball and dissected the attributes that made Real Madrid, Barcelona and Inter Milan so superior in European competition.

Then Cantwell came to United, supposedly a far bigger club than his previous employers, only to find petty arguments over a practice kit deemed not fit for tramps or paupers. He would complain about everything: the preparation was beyond contempt, there were no tactics or talk of defensive formations. Set-piece moves seemed an anathema and in the manic training sessions players appeared content to kick lumps out of each other. It all came to a head when criticism of trainer and former United goalkeeper Jack Crompton went too far.

Crompton implored Busby to intervene. It was explained to Cantwell there was the "*United way*" or the door. Soon the sophisticated Irishman and his sky high West Ham ideals settled down to become an integral part of the new Manchester United. So much so that in time Busby made him Captain. Whilst Cantwell was a thorn in the management's side, he clearly had a point. There were others, though who needed to be weeded out of the Old Trafford dressing room.

Disturbing stories were being whispered…

Infrequent tales of match-fixing surfaced during that period between 1960 and 1962. It was the ultimate, unforgivable sin and signalled that defeat no longer hurt United players, quite the opposite. Unexpected hammerings, such as a notorious 7-2 mauling at Newcastle, caused eyebrows to be raised. Events came to a head one sad Saturday at Highbury when certain United players appeared disgusted at a team mate when he scored and it all nearly became public knowledge when *Daily Mail* journalists confronted goalkeeper Harry Gregg. It was quickly explained to the volatile Irishman he was not involved, but that it was clear others were guilty. The players involved were household names whom would have been lynched in Manchester had they been outed. The shocked United goalkeeper had his long running suspicions confirmed and was sick to the stomach. Gregg knew there was only one man who could put things right.

"I knew it! I just bloody knew it" raged Busby, when Gregg confronted him. The United goalkeeper suspected that his manager had an inkling but needed genuine proof. A meeting was called of all the playing staff, the reason unclear. There were worried faces as rumours persisted that something big was going down.

Surely the boss had not found out?

In came Busby flanked by Jimmy Murphy and Jack

Crompton. The atmosphere was intense. Pulling a letter from his pocket, Busby read out a letter of apology he had received from the editor of the *Daily Mail* for the behaviour of his two reporters in Blackpool regarding their *"incorrect"* allegation against United players throwing matches. Matt Busby had called in every favour to extract this apology from the Mail. The guilty had got the message.

The boss knew and it would happen no more.

On Saturday 5th May 1963, Manchester United made the short journey across town to take on City, in undoubtedly their most important match since Sheffield Wednesday had to be overcome in Munich's grim aftermath. Both clubs had three games left to play and were seemingly trapped in a spider's web incapable of escaping the bottom of the table, unless one used the other for leverage to jump clear. 52,000 had claimed their place on the terraces hours before kick-off, as outside chaos reigned on Maine Road's forecourt. Thousands attempted to gate-crash by wrenching open the stadium's main doors in a mad rush to watch what threatened to be a relegation death knell for whoever lost. To the absolute joy of Manchester's blue side, the player who had grabbed a last gasp Old Trafford winner in a 3-2 victory earlier in the season, struck again after just eight minutes to ignite Maine Road. Twenty-three-year-old Scotsman Alex Harley, looked to have handed his team a lifeline and at the same time doom United. Harley should have scored again shortly after, only for United's reserve goalkeeper David Gaskell, standing in for injured Harry Gregg, to deny him from point blank range. It was an occasion full of tension and petty fouls. A war of attrition broke out. The visitors attack led by Bobby Charlton, Denis Law and David Herd were being denied by blue shirted defenders, throwing body and heart in to deny United.

Passions ran high and fists flew; none more so than in the tunnel at half time when United's latest signing, former Celtic's midfield schemer Paddy Crerand, punched City defender David Wagstaff to the floor for a comment made during play. On being challenged by a member of City's backroom staff the fiery Scot warned him that he could expect similar treatment, only for the person in question to quickly disappear through a Maine Road side door. A furious Matt Busby confronted Crerand in the visitor's dressing room. When asked outright if he had floored Wagstaff,

Crerand vehemently denied it!

Signed on the infamous date of 6th February 1963, exactly five years after Munich, Paddy Crerand was the type of character both on and off the pitch that the United manager had sought since the crash and was crying out for. A no-nonsense, trustworthy, loyal lieutenant who would never back down when the boots were flying. He possessed a passionate will to win that sometimes overstepped the mark as many opponents would discover in time. Though what charmed Busby most was his vivid imagination and wonderful passing, both short and long. Though hardly blessed with pace it mattered little, for Paddy Crerand was quicker in mind than most and became an integral part of any United team sent out by Busby as the sixties unfolded. As for the unfortunate Wagstaff, his day would only get worse.

The second half wore on with United becoming increasingly desperate for an equaliser. Six minutes remained when Maine Road erupted in controversy. Wagstaff under hit a back pass towards goalkeeper Harry Dowd and the ball was chased down by Denis Law, whose ankles appeared to be grabbed as he tumbled over. As the blue majority of the crowd howled and screamed venom at Law, the referee Mr McCabe awarded a penalty. Showing great bravery when other team-mates turned their backs, Albert Quixall, a player many Old Trafford supporters remained unsure of, fired past Dowd, to secure the point that ultimately saved United and relegated City.

And yet,

just three days later Matt Busby's master under

achievers almost blew it at home to Leyton Orient. At half time they trailed 1-0 to former legendary United captain Johnny Carey's team. Again, the 33,000 people present were being made to sweat and boos swept around Old Trafford. Early in the second half a Bobby Charlton cross was turned into his own net by Bobby's namesake, Orient defender Stan Charlton's diving header. It was an equaliser that did little to change moods on the terraces as they waited in trepidation for their team to slip up again. Once more the air was fraught with uncertainty until the last ten minutes, when Denis Law pounced to soothe red brows. Then, as news filtered through from Upton Park of Manchester City being savaged 6-1 at West Ham, to confirm their plight Bobby Charlton smashed a third United goal to end all doubts. Manchester United were staying up and all thought could now turn to their forthcoming appearance in the 1963 FA Cup final.

The winter of 1962-63 had been the worst any could remember and the backlog of fixtures meant there was little football played between Christmas and February. United were forced into playing eight games in a manic March including three FA Cup ties and, as their league form continued to drive both Busby and Murphy to distraction, suddenly, without really thinking they were in the cup semi-finals.

On Saturday 27th April 1963, United took on second division giant killers Southampton at Villa Park, and in a grim semi-final clash that few remember with any fondness, Denis Law struck after twenty-two minutes to clinch a Wembley appearance. For Matt Busby the opportunity had arisen to show the world that his efforts to rebuild Manchester United were starting to take shape. A team that tried to play football in a manner befitting the memory of those lost at Munich. In Charlton, Law and Crerand the manager felt he had the bedrock of greatness. Only time would tell.

After finishing fourth to complete their best ever league season, Leicester started favourites to win the cup. If not spectacular they were hard working and difficult to beat. The type of First Division team that Manchester United so often struggled against and yet even though fourteen positions separated the two sides, the mantle of under-dogs did not sit well with United players and supporters.

Matt Busby had selection problems, notably with Nobby Stiles who had suffered a hamstring pull in the recent Manchester derby. United's plight that day was such Stiles played on in considerable agony, thus aggravating the injury and all but ruling him out of Wembley. Into the side came Stiles' best friend and future brother-in-law Johnny Giles. In terms of natural talent, Giles was arguably the best player at Old Trafford, but a tetchy relationship with Busby meant this dark haired, tough but technically gifted little Irishman would soon seek footballing solace away from Manchester. He was later to haunt the United manager for ten years at Don Revie's up and coming Leeds.

In attempting to rebuild after Munich, Busby had never been afraid to spend big and his side that took to the field at Wembley back in 1963 cost in the region of £300,000. By far the most expensive team to reach an FA cup final. The quality of footballer available to Busby was the highest since the crash and if they clicked on the day capable of giving anyone a game. Twenty minutes before kick-off drama occurred in the United dressing room when it was discovered Paddy Crerand had disappeared. In his eagerness to witness the crowd singing along with the band, *"Abide with me"* the traditional cup final hymn, a curious Crerand had gone walkabout to stand in the tunnel. There he watched the pomp and ceremony unfold. On returning, a frantic Busby quizzed his fellow Scotsman, before the bell rang and it was officially time to enter the pitch.

Led by Captain Noel Cantwell, Manchester United stepped back onto the Wembley turf for the first time since 1958. Football writers predicted widely that Leicester's strong defence would deliver for the trophy and send it to Filbert Street.

With the highly rated twenty-six-year-old Gordon
Banks in goal, and a defence marshalled superbly
by their commanding Scottish centre-half and
captain Frank Mclintock, they claimed Leicester
were more than capable of handling the high-
explosive concoction of Law, Herd and Charlton.
Whilst at the other end of the pitch, United's much
discussed Achilles heel, their own rearguard, was
deemed likely to concede against a nun's eleven.

At first, all talk of a spectacle looked to have
been muted as Leicester's tactics appeared to be sit
back and play on the break. Indeed, early on eight
white shirts stood in their own penalty area as
United's Maurice Setters took possession still
inside his own half? When the *Foxes* did move
forward the uncertainty in the Mancunian defence
shown itself to be a curse that at any time could
prove their undoing. No more than goalkeeper
David Gaskell. Three times in a mistake-littered
opening fifteen minutes, the error-prone Gaskell
flapped to present Leicester players with clear cut
opportunities, only for centre-forward Ken
Keyworth and his fellow strikers to miss them.
Having survived United breathed heavy. Wembley
was hard on both legs and minds. Bill Foulkes for
one experiencing cup final nerves. He, along with
Bobby Charlton, were the only crash survivors left
in the starting eleven. The sheer emotion of an
already draining occasion and the pressure to

finally win silverware after Munich taking a heavy toll.

United hit back, Denis Law's menace and guile played in Albert Quixall with a superb pass. Quixall's inability to control allowed Banks to dive courageously at his feet and clear the danger. Nevertheless, orchestrated by a probing Crerand, United built an incessant passing rhythm, they dominated possession, their football neat and incisive. Bobby Charlton went soaring through and unleashed a typical rasping effort that Gordon Banks did well to save. Banks' ensuing kick out to Scottish inside-right Dave Gibson was robbed by fellow countryman Paddy Crerand. A typical act of swift thinking saw Crerand intercept, and spot Denis Law arriving in the penalty area. Law got the ball ten yards out and with his back to goal let the pass run behind him, turned and then in an eye blink lashed a low shot past Banks into the net. Manchester United led and their mass travelling support went mad. On the bench Busby was up celebrating but a season long torment meant any thought of victory remained folly, for he knew his team was capable of anything – good or bad. Shortly before half time it should have been 2-0 when the scintillating Law sped like a red blur past Banks, shot goal wards and missed by an inch. It was all United, their play calm and progressive. Leicester were rocked as the interval came, yet remained only a goal down and the game was anything but over. The second-half saw a brief flurry from the Midlands club and a still shaky Gaskell dropped the ball at the feet of onrushing City midfielder Graham Cross, who inexplicably shot wide. Sadly, for their supporters whom tried in vain to rouse Leicester, they fell back into a first half mode of careless passing, and on fifty-seven minutes paid a heavy price. A long goal kick by Gaskell found the cunning Johnny Giles lurking wide-right. A touch of class followed as he beat his man before flighting a precision cross-field pass to an unmarked Bobby Charlton. Racing with deadly intent into the box Charlton let fly a shot straight at Gordon Banks. As Wembley held its breath the Leicester goalkeeper failed to hold and United striker David Herd swept the ball home.

Across the Wembley terraces a sea of red simply exploded in delight. A victorious, deafening chorus of *"When the reds go marching in"* erupted amongst them. With United so on top it felt already that the cup was won. As Paddy Crerand controlled the centre of the pitch with a calm but tough authority and Albert Quixall alongside having undoubtedly his finest match since arriving at Old Trafford, even Matt Busby appeared relatively content. He should have known better for from seemingly down and out Leicester struck back. Ten minutes from time Keyworth's diving header beat Gaskell's flailing fingers to cut the deficit and reignite City hopes. Suddenly, the Leicester faithful raised the volume and the 1963 FA Cup final was back on. Stunned but determined not to throw the cup away United roared back. Denis Law switched play to David Herd then sprinted forty yards forward into the penalty area for the expected return. When it came the 'Lawman' smashed a brilliant arcing header past a desperate Banks, only for the ball to agonisingly hit the post and roll rather shamefully back into Bank's grateful hands. Ever the showman Law, in mock histrionics, collapsed to the floor.

On eighty-five minutes all doubts vanished when from another precise Johnny Giles cross, Denis Law jumped with Gordon Banks, who for the second time erred and dropped the ball at the feet of David Herd. Taking aim, a prowling Herd took advantage and flashed a skimming drive past two desperate Leicester defenders trying to block on the goal-line.

At 3-1 there was unbridled ecstasy amongst the red hordes. The cup was going to Manchester and six long painful years after Munich, the Mancunians could once more glimpse silverware. Even when Captain Noel Cantwell threw the cup high, few worried he would not catch it on the way down. For on that sunlit Wembley afternoon it had been United's day. When interviewed after the match by the BBC's David Coleman, Busby claimed, "Having so many big time players won us the cup." As for Leicester City, their manager Matt Gilles spoke for thousands of United supporters when he said, "I can't understand how they can play like that today and finish where they did in the league?"

Free from the lament of a trophy less period, there now existed a fervent hope of better days ahead. Mancunians revelled in glory. On returning home a city ignited in joy at being back amongst the land of the living. Hundreds of thousands lined the streets and pavements. Every sightseeing vantage was taken. People hung off lamp posts, on top of bus shelters. Others climbed rather warily onto high narrow window ledges. The bus carrying the victorious United team edged its way at snail's pace, showing off a trophy that was so much more than a simple prize. Munich still cut deep, those lost never to be forgotten but now,

life could go on.

On entering its final destination for a civic reception at the town hall, the bus went under a huge man-made red and white arch. A moment in time perhaps that signified when Manchester United had moved on from the end of that southern German runway. No longer did their supporters feel guilty at looking forward. As Matt Busby raised the cup high to the ecstatic crowds in Albert Square it was clear United were back.

POST NOTE: Five years later when Manchester United finally achieved their rainbow's end, a journey laced with tears culminated with a 4-1 win over Benfica in the European cup final at Wembley. Waiting for them that night on returning to the dressing room was a telegram. On it read…Congratulations from your friends in Madrid.

Don Santiago Bernabéu…

In today's much more cynical and high-powered footballing environment, such acts appear more than a lifetime ago. Sir Alex Ferguson's comments, 'I wouldn't sell that lot a virus' when Real were trying to tempt Cristiano Ronaldo to Madrid shown a once close relationship was well and truly a thing of the past. Maybe so, the sad truth being this particular tale of two cities belongs now to a different era. However, those United supporters knowledgeable of this story will never forget such generosity of spirt by Real Madrid, whom when their club was at its lowest ever ebb came to help.

Sometimes,

you simply cannot buy class.

Don Santiago Bernabéu lays flowers on Eddie Colman's grave.

THE END

John Ludden
All Rights Reserved:

Printed by Amazon Italia Logistica S.r.l.
Torrazza Piemonte (TO), Italy

10511264R00058